FATHER KNOWS BEST

Great Quotations Publishing Company

Compiled by Peggy Schaffer
Cover Art and Design by Jeff Maniglia
Typeset and Design by Caroline Solarski and Julie Otlewis

© 1995 Great Quotations Publishing Company

All rights reserved.
Written permission must be secured from the publisher
to use or reproduce any part of this book,
except for brief quotations in critical reviews or articles.

Published by Great Quotations Publishing Company,
1967 Quincy Court
Glendale Heights, Illinois 60139

ISBN: 1-56245-068-9

Printed in Hong Kong

The more a child becomes aware of a father's willingness to listen, the more a father will begin to hear.

— Gordon MacDonald

A family is a unit composed not only of children, but of fathers, mothers, an occasional animal and at times, the common cold.

— Ogden Nash

A young branch takes on all the bends that one gives to it.

— Chinese Proverb

For the father of a little-leaguer,
a baseball game is simply a nervous breakdown into innings.

— Earl Wilson

For many little girls, life with
father is a dress rehearsal for love and marriage.

— David Jeremiah

Fathers can shape their children's understanding of their mothers by loving them deeply.

— James Dobson

It may be hard on some fathers not to have a son,
but it is much harder on a boy not to have a father.

— Sara Gilbert

When a girl hits thirteen,
you can just watch her lose her mind.
Luckily, she gets it back;
but during the time that it's misplaced,
you can lose your own.

— Bill Cosby

A child should be loved for who he is,
not for what he does.

— David Jeremiah

My father was not a failure.
He was, after all, the father
of a president of the United States.

— Harry S. Truman

Dads, write your grown children a letter
to express your love.
Maybe even a confession or two
of how you wished you'd done more with them
might be appropriate.

Many a man spanks his children
for things his own father should have spanked him for.

— Don Marquis

When your fifteen-year-old son does speak,
he often says one of two things:
either "okay," which,
as we all know, means,
"I haven't killed anybody," or, "no problem".

— Bill Cosby

I owe almost everything to my father.

— Margaret Thatcher

Dads, take a walk together with your children. Just talk about the "stuff" of their lives.

A boy is a magical creature--
you can lock him out of your workshop,
but you can't lock him out of your heart.

— Alan Beck

Parents of teens and parents of babies
have something in common.
They spend a great deal of time trying to
get their kids to talk.

— Paul Swets

Sincere compliments from father to daughter, can build her self-esteem as few other things can.

We should measure affection,
not by the ardor of its passion,
but by its strength and constancy.

— Cicero

He has far to flee
who flees from his own family.

I talk and talk,
and I haven't taught people in fifty years
what my father taught by example in one week.

— Mario Cuomo

Level with your child by being honest.
Nobody spots a phony quicker than a child.

— M. MacCracken

A father's character
provides the basis of how he leads.

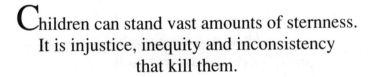

Children can stand vast amounts of sternness.
It is injustice, inequity and inconsistency
that kill them.

— Father Robert Capon

All children alarm their fathers,
if only because you are forever expecting
to encounter yourself.

— Gore Vidal

If you keep telling your son something's wrong with him,
sooner or later he'll believe it.
Follow every, "That's wrong",
by saying what's right.

— John E. Anderson

Reasoning with a child is fine,
if you can reach the child's reason
without destroying your own.

— John Mason Brown

Parents must get across the idea that,
"I love you always,
but sometimes I do not love your behavior."

— Amy Vanderbilt

I never understood the obstacles my father faced,
until I became one.
I love my father's memory now more than ever.

Other things may change us,
but we start and end with the family.

— Anthony Brandt

Love children especially...
they live to soften and purify our hearts.
Woe to him who offends a child.

— Feodor Dostoevsky

The best gift a father can give his child
is the gift of himself.

When I was as you are now,
towering the confidence of twenty-one,
I did not suspect that I should be
at forty-nine what I am now.

— Samuel Johnson

Where can one better be than the bosom of one's own family.

The husband who makes no mistakes does not normally make anything.

— Edward Phelps

The value of marriage is not that adults produce children
but that children produce adults.

— Peter DeVries

Children who despise their parents
do so until about age forty,
when they suddenly become like them.

— Quentin Crewe

Dad, your little boy is your captor, your jailer,
your boss and your master--
a freckle-faced, pint-sized, cat-chasing
bundle of noise.

— Alan Beck

If it is desirable that children be kind,
appreciative, and pleasant,
then those qualities should be taught--
not hoped for.

— James Dobson

Family life is an existential classroom that lasts about eighteen years.

— Gordon MacDonald

Midlife crisis is that moment when you realize your children and your clothes are about the same age.

— Bill Tammeus

'Tis a happy thing
to be a father unto many sons.

— William Shakespeare

Before I got married
I had six theories about bringing up children;
now I have six children and no theories.

— Lord Rochester

He was not merely a chip off the old block, but the old block itself!

— Edmund Burke

A child's hand in yours--
what tenderness and power it arouses.
You are instantly the very touchstone of
wisdom and strength.

— Marjorie Holms

By profession I am a soldier
and take pride in that fact,
but I am prouder to be a father.

— General Douglas MacArthur

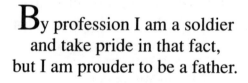

The family is one of nature's masterpieces.

— George Santayana

Many a father wishes he were strong enough
to tear a telephone book in two--
especially if he has a teenage daughter.

— Guy Lombardo

Fathers, train your children in their youth and they won't train you in your old age.

Truth, which is important to a scholar,
has got to be concrete.
And there's nothing more concrete
than dealing with babies,
burps, bottles and frogs.

— Jeane Kirkpatrick

A father ought to help his son to form the habit
of doing right on his own initiative
rather than out of fear of serious consequences.

— Terence

Dad, when you come home at night
with only shattered pieces of your dreams,
your little one can mend them like new
with two magic words--
"Hi, Dad!"

— Alan Beck

Always the same hard-working dad,
 plodding day after day;
Thereby ready to meet all the bills
 that are ever around to be paid.

You don't choose your family.
They are God's gift to you,
as you are to them.

— Desmond Tutu

We need good fathers in our homes
whose hearts are full of grace.
Who by their love and earnest prayers,
make home a pleasant place.

— Walter Isenhour

An important thing for parents to teach
their children is how to get along without them.

— F. Clark

Be kind to thy father,
for when thou wert young,
who loved thee so fondly as he?

— Margaret Courtney

Performance under stress
is one test of effective leadership.
It may also be the proof of accomplishment
when it comes to evaluating the quality of a father.

— Gordon MacDonald

Make me, kind Lord, a worthy dad,
   that I may lead this little lad.
 In pathways ever fair and bright,
   that I may keep his steps aright.

Somehow, when you're a child,
you simply accept each turn of events as it comes,
as if there is no other way for the world to be.

— Isabel Huggan

One father is worth more
than one hundred school masters.

— G. Herbert

Remember, when your child has a tantrum, don't have one of your own.

— Dr. J. Kuriansky

The imprint of the father remains forever
on the life of the child.

Children miss nothing in sizing up their parents. If you are only half convinced of your beliefs, they will quickly discern that fact.

— James Dobson

A girl's father is the first man in her life
and probably the most influential.

— David Jeremiah

A boy's will is the wind's will
and the thoughts of youth are long, long thoughts.

— Henry Wadsworth Longfellow

Dear and good--dependable dad,
   always so steady and true;
   a man of few words--
   he never says much,
   unless there is really need to.

It's easier for a father to have children
than for children to have a real father.

— M Turnbull

Parents learn a lot from their children about coping with life.

— Muriel Spark

A father should never make distinctions between his children.

— The Talmud

The joys of mothers and fathers are secret,
and so are their griefs and fears.

— Francis Bacon

When I was a kid,
I used to imagine animals running under my bed.
I told my dad,
and he solved the problem by cutting off the legs of the bed.

— Lou Brock

Allow children to be happy their own way;
for what better way will they ever find?

— Dr. Samuel Johnson

Opportunities for meaningful communication between fathers and sons must be created. And it's work to achieve.

— James Dobson

Daughters will perceive how women should
be treated (or not treated)
according to how dad treats mother and other women.

— David Jeremiah

My daddy doesn't work, he just goes to the office;
but sometimes he does errands on the way home.

A child tells in the street what its father says at home.

— The Talmud

A father is a thing that is forced to endure childbirth without an anesthetic.

— Paul Harvey

U̲nless a father accepts his faults
he will most certainly doubt his virtues.

— Hugh Prather

Lucky is the man
whose children make his happiness in life.

— Euripides

Never help a child with a task at which he feels he can succeed.

— M. Montessori

We never know the love of the parent
until we become parents ourselves.

— Henry Ward Beecher

Small children can disturb your sleep,
big children your life.

— Yiddish Proverb

If you want your child to accept your values
when he reaches his teen years,
then you must be worthy of his respect
during his younger days.

— James Dobson

If a father would have a trustworthy son,
he must give occasion to trust him.

A wonderful motto for teens and parents
is to never needlessly harm the respect of another.

— Dr. Kay Kuzma

The character and history of each child
may be a new and poetic experience to the parent,
if he will let it.

— Margaret Fuller

Making terms with reality, with things as they are,
is a full-time business for the child.

— Milton Sapirstein

A father is a thing that growls
when it feels good...
and laughs very loud
when it's scared half to death.

— Paul Harvey

A little child, a limber self.
Singing dancing to itself...
Makes such a vision to the sight,
as fills a father's eyes with light.

— S. T. Coleridge

One of the closest bonds
a father can have with his daughter
comes through comforting.

— David Jeremiah

Is it not strange
that he who has no children
brings them up so well?

— Confucius

A father has the opportunity to choose his words,
but he cannot always control the consequences
that his words create.

— Gordon MacDonald

Like father like son:
every good tree maketh good fruits.

— William Langland

The most important relationship within the family,
second only to that of husband and wife,
is the relationship between father and daughter.

— David Jeremiah

While we criticize the fathers for being narrow. we should not forget that they were also deep.

— William Foulkes

Children have never been very good
at listening to their fathers
but they never fail to imitate them.

— James Baldwin

I was the same kind of father
as I was a harpist--I played by ear.

— Harpo Marx

...some day you will be old enough
to start reading fairy tales again.

— C. S. Lewis

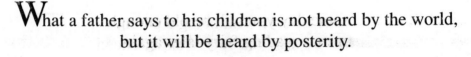

What a father says to his children is not heard by the world, but it will be heard by posterity.

— Jean Paul Richter

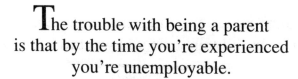

The trouble with being a parent is that by the time you're experienced you're unemployable.

— H. Less

Let your children go if you want to keep them.

— M. Forbes

It's not flesh and blood,
but the heart that makes us fathers and sons.

— S. Chiller

I could not point to any need in childhood as strong as that for a father's protection.

— S Freud

Everyone knows a great deal about one child--himself.

— Brad Carter

Build me a son, O Lord,
who will be strong enough
to know when he is weak--
and brave enough
to face himself in honest defeat.

— General Douglas MacArthur

What children hear at home soon flies abroad.

— Thomas Fuller

We need good fathers o'er the land,
who live and tell the truth.
And have at heart along life's way,
the welfare of our youth.

— Walter E Isenhour

He that has his father for judge goes safe to the trial.

— Cervantes

A happy childhood can't be cured.
Mine'll hang around my neck like a rainbow,
that's all, instead of a noose.

No man is really depraved who can spend half an hour
by himself on the floor
playing with his little boy's electric train.

— Simeon Strunsky

He who lies to his father,
will be all the more daring
in attempting the same with others.

— Terence

The ultimate test of a relationship is to disagree but to hold hands.

— Alexandra Penny

A father's love is for his children
and the children's love for their children.

— The Talmud

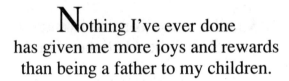

Nothing I've ever done
has given me more joys and rewards
than being a father to my children.

— Bill Cosby

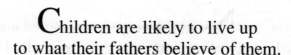

Children are likely to live up to what their fathers believe of them.

— Lady Bird Johnson

Your work was waste?
Maybe your share lay in the hour you laughed and kissed.
Who knows but that your son shall wear the laurels
that his father missed.

— Laurence Hope

What a distressing contrast there is
between the radiant intelligence of the child
and the feeble mentality of the average adult.

— S. Freud

In order to form lives,
we must stop being speakers
and start being fathers.

— Juan Carlos Ortiz

Boys will be boys,
and so will a lot of middle-aged men.

— F. M. Hubbard

Sons forget what grandsons wish to remember.
— Alice Rossi

Old boys have their playthings
as well as young ones;
the difference is only in the price.

— Benjamin Franklin

The most important thing a father can do for his children is to love their mother.

— Theodore M. Hesburgh

A boy with head enough to amount to anything in the world can't help wondering how he is going to do it when everybody tells him how much like his father he is.

If youth is a defect, it is one we outgrow too soon.

— Robert Lowell

Dad works so very hard,
to buy nice things for mother.
And after dinner in the yard,
he plays with me and brother.

— Alvery E. Ford

An infallible way to make your child miserable
is to satisfy all his demands.

A father is a fellow
who has replaced the currency in his wallet
with snapshots of his kids.

—- Mike Forest

How easily a father's tenderness is recalled
and how quickly a son's offenses vanish
at the slightest word of repentance!

— Moliere

We had bad luck with our kids--
they've all grown up.

— Christopher Morley

When I was a boy of fourteen,
my father was so ignorant
I could hardly stand to have him around.
But when I got to be twenty-one,
I was astonished at how much the old man had learned.

— Mark Twain

That men will never be unwelcome to others who makes himself agreeable to his own family.

— Platus

You don't raise heroes, you raise sons.
And if you treat them like sons,
they'll turn out to be heroes.

— Walter Schirra

Build me a son whose heart will be clear,
whose goal will be high--
a son who will master himself
before he seeks to master others.

— General Douglas MacArthur

There must always be a struggle
between a father and a son,
while one aims at power
the other at independence.

— Samuel Johnson

Fathers are what give daughters away
to other men who aren't nearly good enough...
so they can have grandchildren
that are smarter than anybody's.

— Paul Harvey

If a dad and his son can develop hobbies together
or other common interests,
the rebellious years can pass in relative tranquility.

— James Dobson

A man who has faults he doesn't know about probably doesn't listen to his wife.

It now costs more to amuse a child
than it once did to educate his father.

— H. V. Prochnow

Words have an awesome impact.
The impressions made by a father's voice
can set in motion an entire trend of life.

— Gordon MacDonald

Praise your children openly,
reprove them secretly.

— W. Cecil

A real family man is one who looks at his new child
as an addition
rather than a deduction.

You can do anything with children
if you only play with them.

— Otto Von Bismarck

I have found the happiness of parenthood greater than any other that I have experienced.

— Bertrand Russell

"My son!"
What simple, beautiful words!
"My boy!"
What a wonderful phrase.

— Cyril Morton Thorne

A new father quickly learns
that his child comes to the bathroom at the wrong times.
The only way for this father to be certain of bathroom privacy
is to shave at the gas station.

— Bill Cosby

My dad and I hunted and fished together.
How could I get angry at this man
who took the time to be with me?

— James Dobson

In bringing up children,
what good mothers and fathers
instinctively feel like doing for their babies
is usually best after all.

— Benjamin Spock

If I am an effective father
it is because I have devoted myself to become
an instrument and model
of human experience to my children.

— Gordon MacDonald

A torn jacket is soon mended;
but hard words bruise the heart of a child.

— Henry Wadsworth Longfellow

Train your child in the way in which you know you should have gone yourself.

— C. H. Spurgeon

Words which explode at an impressionable moment
in the life of a young child,
can shape an entire personality.

— Gordon MacDonald

Children are a great comfort in your old age.
And they help you reach it sooner too.

— Lionel M. Kauffman

When you are dealing with a child,
keep all your wits about you,
and sit on the floor.

— A. O'Malley

Dad's going to take us fishing;
he promised yesterday.
He knows the pools and shallows,
where trout and catfish play.

— Marjorie Hunt Pettit

Just as the moon is the light of the night
and the sun of the day,
so are good children the light of their father.

I do not love him because he is good,
but because he is my little child.

Wife and children are a kind of
discipline of humanity.

— Francis Bacon

Happy is he that is happy in his children.

— Thomas Fuller

Women make us poets,
children make us philosophers.

— Malcolm De Chazal

Of all nature's gifts to the human race,
what is sweeter to a man than his children?

— Cicero

Our children immediately discern the gap between what we *say* and what we *do*.

Children are our most valuable resource.

— Herbert Hoover

Children are true connoisseurs.
What's precious to them has no price--only value.

— Bel Kaufman

Children are such sticky things, 'specially after tea.

— E. F. Benson

Give love to a little child, and you get a great deal back.

— John Ruskin